MW01114889

THE AMERICAN 'STACHE

To my kids, Ashford and Jones,

Good luck growing a 'stache; your father was never able to.

THE
AMERICAN
'STACHE

Dave Duster

THE
BODACIOUS BOOK COMPANY
MEMPHIS

CONTENTS

'STACHE!

"The Catfish"

"No matter how many fish are in the sea, I'm always the catch of the day."

"The Prom"

"I didn't realize my tie was crooked until the pictures came back."
#Mortified

"The Friday Night"

"I'm a savage on the dance floor."
#MustacheRodeo
#Dangerous
#Giddyup!

"The Barnyard Billionaire"

"All my wives loved my mustache starting out."

"THE VIRGINIA CREEPER"

"Wanted in all 50 states...
by the ladies."

"The Bronx Bro-merang"

"Bringing it all the way back from 1975."

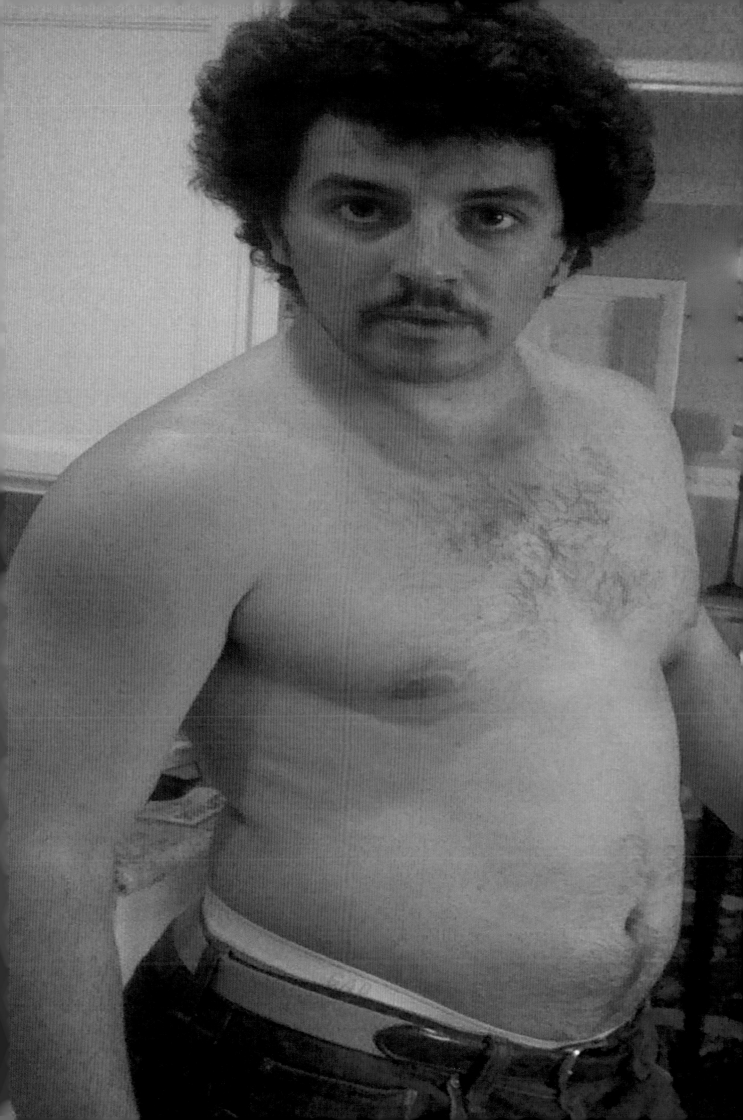

"The Bucket List"

"Wicked 'stache. Check!"

"The Chin Lift"

"My wife says this bad boy
takes 10 years off my face."

"The Grower"

"My eyes are up here, ladies."

"The Smooth Jazz"

"This sweet 'Stache has 'em swaying and swooning into the night."

"The Film Critic"

"Epic! A modern-day masterpiece!"

"The You Can't Date My Daughter"

*"I always have some candy
in my van."*

"The Lip Chap"

"My horse says it's 10 gallons of fun."

"The Love Handle"

"The walrus is my spirit animal."

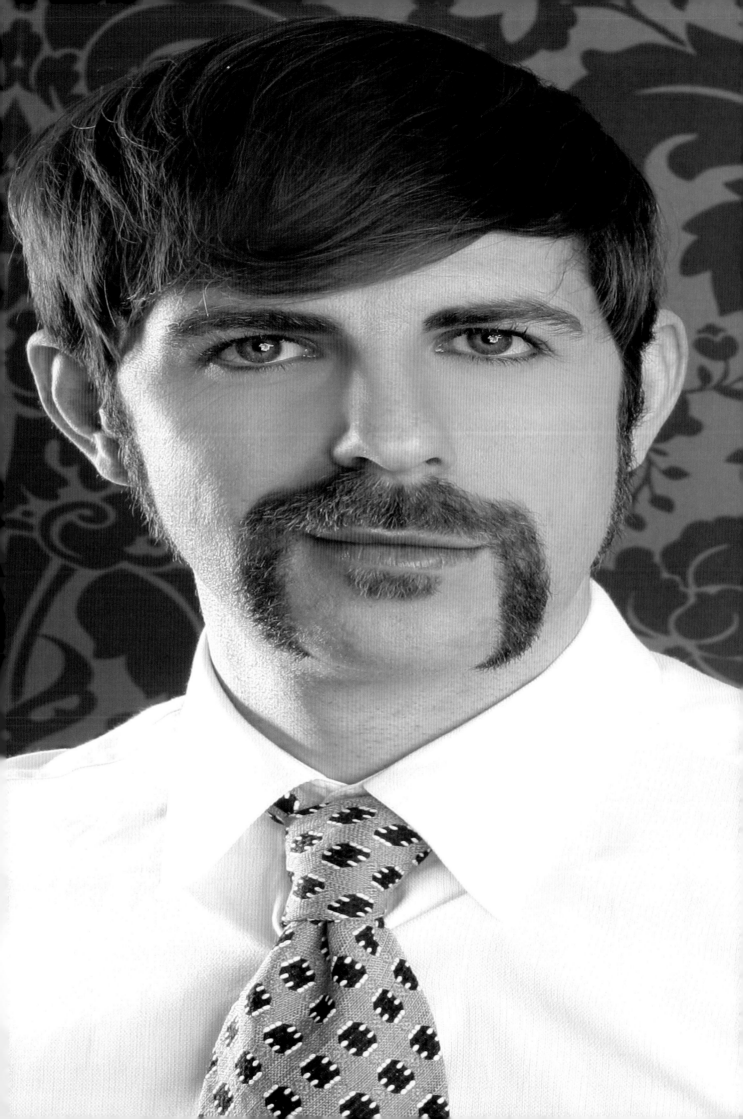

"THE GAME SHOW HOST"

"It doesn't spin, but you always win."

"The Ol' Push Broom"

"When the ladies ask if I have lips under my mustache, I invite them to come find out for themselves."
#Smooth

"The Physician's Assistant"

"The M.D. stands for
Mustache Dominance.
If I could prescribe a 'stache... I would."

"THE LIP BROW"

*"If I smiled any bigger
my mustache would rip in half."*
#HappenedBefore

"The Magician's Apprentice"

"I'll never reveal the spellbinding secrets of my 'stache. It's MUSTAGIC!"

"THE LIPOCTOPUS"

"Makes you wonder what's under the kilt. Amirite?"
#WokeUpLikeThis

"The Hombrella"

*"Not a drop of rain has
touched these lips in 20 years."*

"The .38 Special"

"Tried and true, it always gets the job done."

"THE PRINCIPAL"

"The awesome power of my mustache has been striking fear into the hearts of students for 27 years."

"THE RHODE ISLAND ROLLER COASTER"

"Just roll with it, baby."

"So dedicated to my 30 year 'Stache...
I donated half my left eyebrow
to my upper lip."

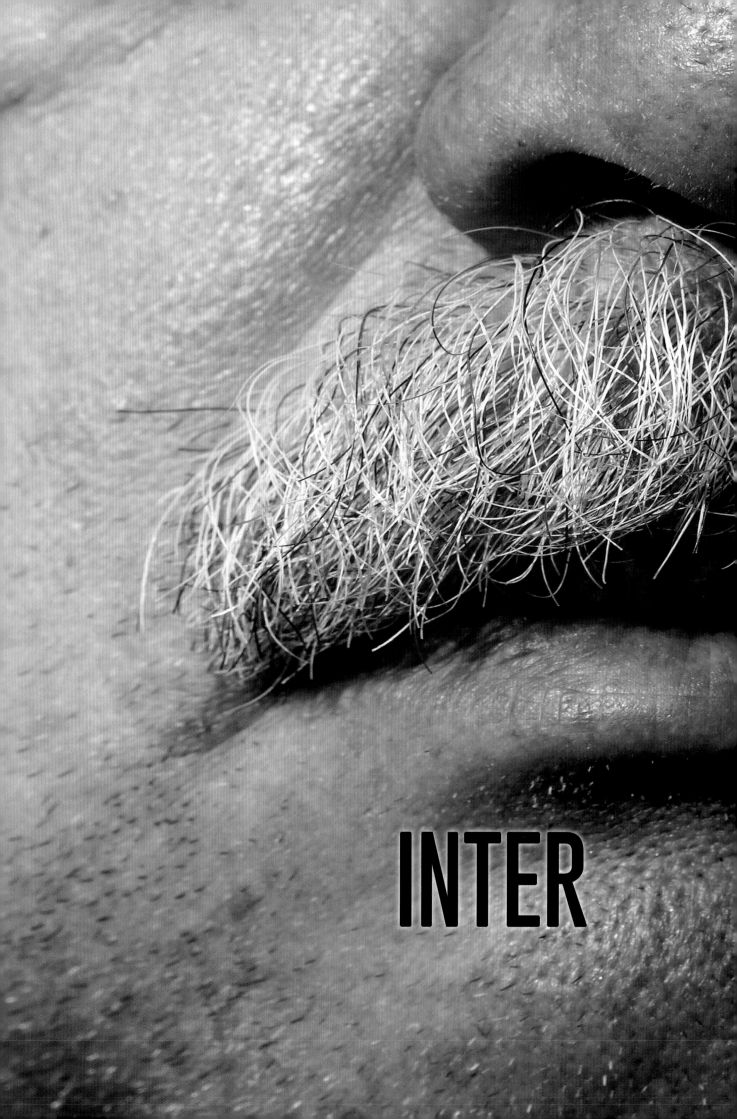

INTER

MISSION

"The Pony Express"

*"This ol' lip duster delivers
seven days a week."*

"The Angry Drill Sergeant"

"Never give me a clean shave. Ever."

"The Lip Jacket"

"The winters get cold on my scooter. Gotta keep that upper lip warm."

"The Lip o' Luxury"

"I live vicariously through my 'stache."

"The Offensive Line"

"More practice, girls. More practice."

"El Capitán"

"Some sail by the stars, but my mo' is my compass."

"The Portland Poet"

"I express my feelings through words... and facial hair."

"The Old Bullet Proof"

"My neighbors say when I'm not upset...I'm really a pretty nice guy."

"THE SOUTHWEST SECRET KEEPER"

"You can tell me anything. I'm a master at keeping it under my hat... and my spicy flavor saver."

"THE SHOCK AND AWE"

"Every day just gets better than the last."

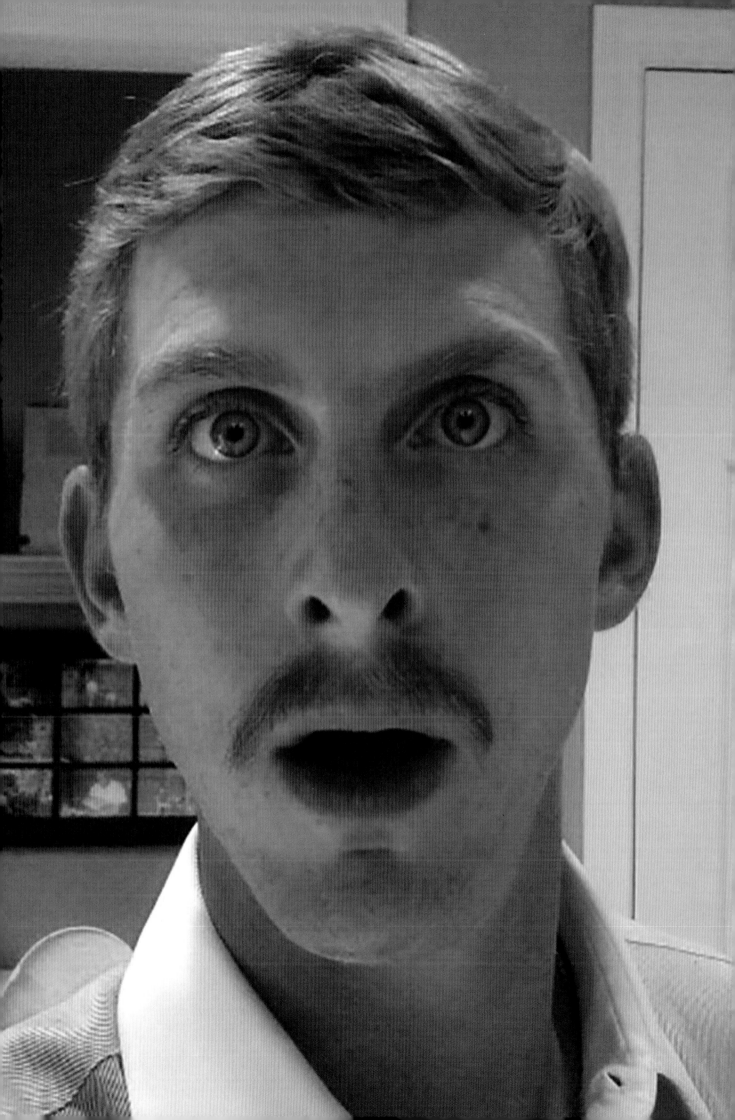

"The Artist"

"A true mo' will stir your emotions and your paint."

"Mustache wax is the key to my heart."

"The Middle-Aged Divorcé"

" The hair says 'responsible'. The 'stache says 'wild and free!' "

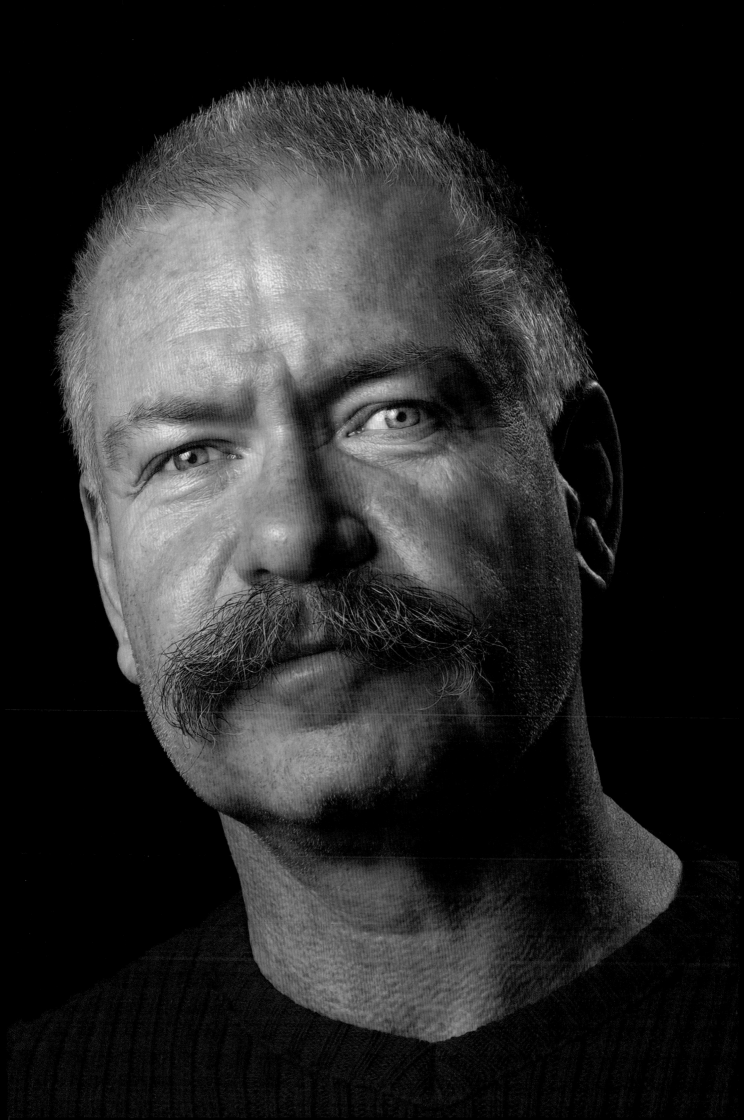

"The Perpetual Happiness"

"Even on rough days, my mustache is still smiling."

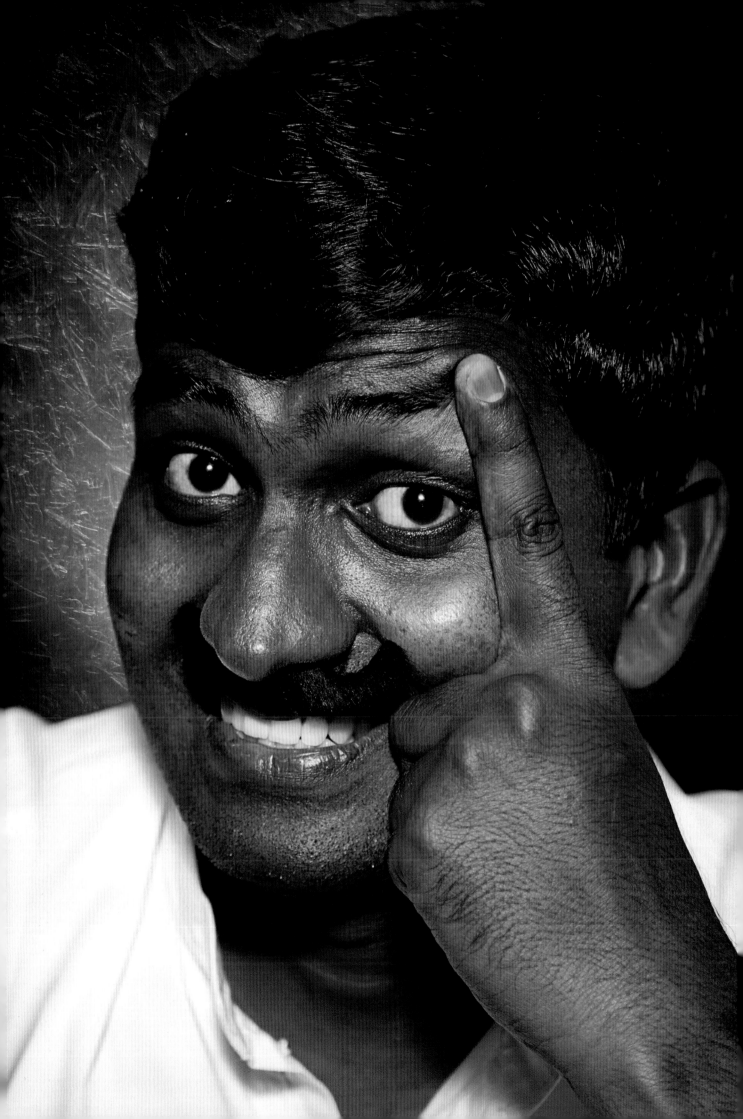

"The Hip Tennis Instructor"

"For the love of the game!"

"The Tennessee Tough Love"

"When it comes to life lessons, class is always in session on the Handlebar Highway."

"THE TOLEDO TRANSPLANT"

"I've always wanted a righteous 'Stache. The ladies are stunned by how natural it looks."
#JustALittleOffTheTop

"THE STEAMPUNK SOPHISTICATE"

"Cell phone salesman by day, suburban air pirate by night."

"The Elder's Wisdom"

"You can tell how intelligent a man is by the width of his mustache. It's true!"

"The Professional"

"It's business doing pleasure with me."

"THE WIDOW MAGNET"

"This mustache excites the senior dames more than BINGO night!"

"The Boy Band"

"In the cutthroat world of Professional Lip Syncing, a good mustache helps take the focus off of my lips."

"THE CAREER CARNIE"

"Life on the road, it's how I roll."

"The Wisconsin Womanizer"

"My mustache is the best wingman a guy could ask for. The ladies melt like butter."

"The Rebel Yodeler"

"Dress for the job you want, not the one you have."

"The Proud Father"

*"It doesn't scare the kids.
They love it!"*

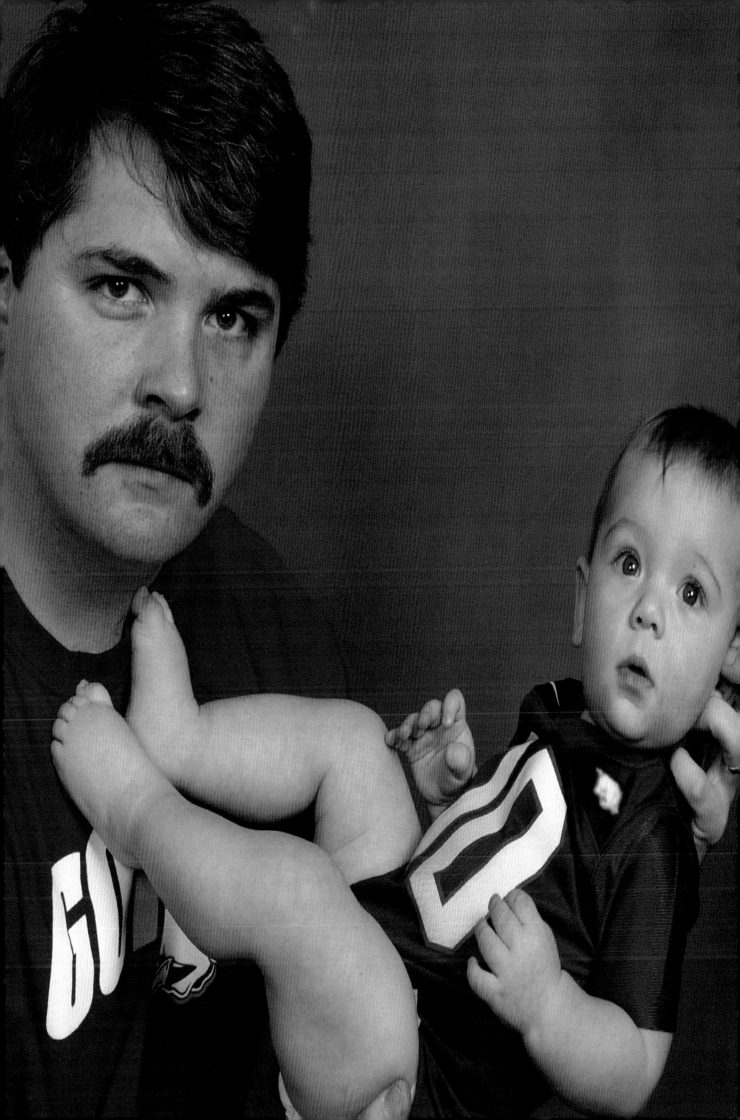

Name Your Own

"   "

"

))

Insert
Stellar 'Stache
Here

A Special Thanks to Jessi
For Helping Bring this Book to Life!